MW01193314

21 DAYS
TO DISCOVER WHO
YOU ARE IN JESUS

LIVING CONFIDENT AND SECURE
IN HIS UNCHANGING
LOVE FOR YOU

By

Connie Witter

HARRISON HOUSE
TULSA, OK

12 11 10 09   10 9 8 7 6 5 4 3 2 1

21 Days To Discover Who You Are in Jesus:
Living Confident and Secure in His Unchanging Love for You
ISBN 13: 978-1-57794-964-0
ISBN 10: 1-57794-964-1
Copyright © 2009 by Connie Witter
PO Box 3064
Broken Arrow, OK 74013
www.conniewitter.com

Published by Harrison House Publishers
PO Box 35035
Tulsa, Oklahoma 74153
www.harrisonhouse.com

Contents

Preface

In a world where you tend to define yourself by the world's standards, you often feel like you don't quite measure up. Insecurity, fear, and lack of confidence are all the result of defining who you are by what people think of you and what you do.

> **It's in Christ that we find out who we are and what we are living for. Long before we first heard of Christ and got our hopes up, he had his eye on us, had designs on us for glorious living, part of the overall purpose he is working out in everything and everyone.**
>
> *Ephesians 1:11,12 MSG*

When you accepted Jesus as your Savior, you became a new person in Christ. You don't have to define yourself by the world's standards anymore. Who you truly are is found in Jesus.

When you know who you are in Jesus and believe it, you'll be transformed from the inside out and you'll live the glorious life that God has planned for you.

You have an enemy who doesn't want your life to glorify God, so just like he did to Eve in the Garden of Eden, he will attempt to deceive you with his lies. This twenty-one day journey will expose the lies the enemy has tried to get you to believe about yourself and reveal the truth of who you truly are in Jesus. As you replace the lies with the truth, you'll live the blessed and happy life that Jesus came to give you. You'll live confident and secure in His unchanging love.

Day 1

I Am Royalty

For He foreordained us (destined us, planned in love for us) to be adopted (revealed) as His own children through Jesus Christ.

Ephesians 1:5 AMP

God loves you so much that He planned to adopt you as His very own child through your faith in Jesus. He chose you because He wanted you to be a part of His royal family. What makes a person royalty? A person is royalty because he or she is a child of a king. Your heavenly Father is the King of kings. When He adopted you as His child, you became a daughter in His kingdom.

But you are a chosen race, a royal priesthood, a dedicated nation, [God's]

own purchased, special people, that you may set forth the wonderful deeds and display the virtues and perfections of Him Who called you out of darkness into His marvelous light.

1 Peter 2:9 AMP

When you became a part of God's royal family, your identity was changed. You went from being a pauper to becoming a princess in the kingdom of God. The King of kings came to live within you, and you became a new person on the inside. You were chosen to display the glory of the One who lives within you. He called you out of the kingdom of darkness and brought you into the kingdom of light.

The kingdom of darkness is the kingdom of Satan. His kingdom is filled with lies. He hates you because you're a child of God. He knows that you're royalty, that you're God's specially purchased daughter.

If you ever really believe the truth about yourself, the glory that lives within you will shine out for the world to see. You'll live victoriously in this world. The devil is afraid of that, so he uses the only weapon he has to keep you feeling defeated—deception. He doesn't want you to know who you are, so he tries to deceive you with his lies. You can always know if you're listening to his lies by how they make your heart feel. The symptoms of believing lies are negative emotions. Discouragement, depression, worry, and fear are all the fruit of believing the devil's lies.

Have you ever heard the devil speak these lies to your heart?

You're nobody special.

You're not important.

You're not good enough.

Jesus came to rescue you from every lie of the enemy. He came to set you free.

> **Always thanking the Father.... For he has rescued us from the kingdom of darkness and transferred us into the Kingdom of his dear Son, who purchased our freedom and forgave our sins.**
>
> *Colossians 1:12-14 NLT*

Everyone used to live in the kingdom of darkness where their sins separated them from God. The Bible says all were sinners and were not a part of God's family. (Eph. 2:11-13.) But Jesus loves you so much that He came as your King and died for your sins. He rose again to rescue you from the kingdom of darkness. When you put your trust in Him, all your sins are forgiven and your identity changes. You're a royal daughter in the kingdom of God.

But just like in the Garden of Eden, your heavenly Father lets you choose who you're going to believe: the lies of the devil or the truth of who you are in Jesus. When you believe Jesus, the fruit of your life is joy, peace, confidence and security.

When I learned what Jesus had done for me and that I am royalty in God's kingdom, I began to look at myself differently. It didn't matter anymore what the world thought or said about me; the only thing that mattered is what Jesus said because He is the Truth. I began to define myself by who I am in Him. I realized that I am chosen, special, forgiven, and perfect in my Father's eyes because of Jesus. I didn't have to believe the lies of the devil anymore. I could believe Jesus and display His glory in the world.

The same is true of you. You're a royal child of God. You don't have to believe the devil's lies anymore. You don't have to define yourself by what the world says or thinks about you. The truth is you are chosen, special, forgiven, and perfect in the Father's eyes because of Jesus. He wants you to see yourself that way too. He's called you to display His glory to the world by believing who you are in Him.

So the next time the enemy attempts to deceive you with his lies, remember who you are in Jesus, and speak the truth out loud:

- I'm a chosen child of the King of kings.
- My sins are forgiven. I'm perfect in my Father's eyes.
- I'm my Father's purchased, special child. I am royalty because of Jesus.

Prayer

Heavenly Father, I know You love me because You sent Jesus to rescue me from the kingdom of darkness and bring me into Your kingdom. Help me to see myself the way You do. The only thing that matters is what You think and say about me. I choose to believe who I am in Jesus. I am chosen, special, and forgiven. I'm royalty because of Jesus.

Day 2

I Am Righteous

I am overwhelmed with joy in the LORD my God! For he has dressed me with the clothing of salvation and draped me in a robe of righteousness. I am like a bridegroom in his wedding suit or a bride with her jewels.

Isaiah 61:10 NLT

When you put your faith in Jesus and accepted His invitation to belong to His royal family, He dressed you in a robe of righteousness. He changed your identity from a sinner into a righteous princess in the kingdom of God. He proved His love by laying His life down for you. When He looks at you, He sees you as justified, innocent, and perfect; and His opinion of you will never change. You have been declared righteous by the blood of Jesus.

> **But God proves His own love for us in that while we were still sinners Christ died for us! …we have now been declared righteous by His blood….**
>
> *Romans 5:8,9 HCSB*

What does it mean to be "declared righteous by His blood"? *Righteous* means to be obedient to all God's commands and to be justified, good, innocent, and perfect in God's sight.

In Deuteronomy 6:25 NLT, God reveals how a person could be declared righteous through the law: "For we will be counted as righteous when we obey all the commands the LORD our God has given us."

Only one man met these conditions of righteousness. His name is Jesus. The Father declared Him righteous because He obeyed every law of God perfectly. He had on a beautiful robe of righteousness. He was justified, good, innocent, and perfect in the Father's sight.

Yet, all of us were sinners. We've all disobeyed God's commands. No matter how hard we try to be good, we've all failed. The Bible says our righteousness is like filthy rags. We were dressed in dirty, sin-stained clothes. Yet Jesus loves us so much that He was willing to take the punishment for our sins. When we put our trust in Him, all our sins were wiped away with His blood. He took off our filthy, sin-stained clothes and dressed us with His righteousness. It was His love gift to us. No matter how hard we tried to be righteous by obeying God's commands, we could never be good enough in our own ability. So, Jesus did it for us.

None of us deserve to be called righteous, that's why it's called a "gift of grace." It's the greatest Christmas gift ever. When Jesus offered it to us and we opened it, inside was a beautiful robe of righteousness. He looked at us with love in His eyes and said, "Let Me dress you with who I am." Now the Father sees us as righteous, good, innocent, and justified because we are in Jesus. Hebrews 10:14 says that Jesus made us perfect forever. The Bible also says:

> **Christ did no wrong thing. But for our sake God put the blame for our wrong ways on Christ. So now God sees us as good, because we are in Christ.**
>
> *2 Corinthians 5:21*
> *WORLDWIDE ENGLISH NT*

Your heavenly Father wants you to exchange *trying for trusting*. I used to try so hard to be good. I wanted to be like Jesus, but because I failed at times, I believed that I wasn't good enough. The devil planted these lies in my mind:

You're not like Jesus.

You need to try harder to be good.

You'll never be good enough.

Then I learned that because I am righteous in Jesus, my heart was set free from believing the lies of the enemy. I didn't have to try anymore in my own strength to be good enough. I was already righteous because of Jesus. When I began to believe who I am in Jesus, He empowered me to act more and more like Him.

You don't have to try anymore in your own strength to be good enough. You can believe the truth that your heavenly Father sees you as good because you are in Christ. Jesus clothed you with His righteousness. It was His wedding gift to you. Now you can agree with what Jesus says about you and realize you are just like Him.

So believe who you are in Jesus. Speak the truth out loud:

- Jesus clothed me with His righteousness. I am just like Him.

- I am good in my Father's eyes because of Jesus.

- Jesus made me perfect forever.

Prayer

Thank You, Jesus, for your love gift to me. I see myself clothed in the robe of righteousness that You purchased for me. You paid a great price so I don't have to look at myself as a sinner anymore. Help me to remember who I am in You. You made me good and perfect in my Father's eyes. I am just like You. Your love for me is amazing!

Day 3

I Am Justified

Therefore, my brothers, I want you to know that through Jesus the forgiveness of sins is proclaimed to you. Through him everyone who believes is justified from everything you could not be justified from by the law of Moses.

Acts 13:38,39 NIV

Not long ago I was thinking about the word *justified*. I had read it many times in my Bible and realized that in Christ, I am justified; but what does it really mean?

I wanted a deeper understanding of who I am in Jesus and what He has provided for me on the cross. I looked up the word *justified* in a Bible dictionary, and this is what I discovered:

"It is the judicial act of God, by which he pardons all the sins of those who believe in Christ, and accounts, accepts, and treats them as righteous in the eye of the law. In addition to the pardon of sin, justification declares that all the claims of the law are satisfied. The law is not relaxed or set aside, but is declared to be fulfilled in the strictest sense; and so the person justified is declared to be entitled to all the advantages and rewards arising from perfect obedience to the law *(Rom. 5:1-10)*.

"It proceeds on the imputing or crediting to the believer by God himself of the perfect righteousness, active and passive, of his Representative and Surety, Jesus Christ *(Rom. 10:3-9)*. Justification is not the forgiveness of a man without righteousness, but a declaration that he possesses a righteousness which perfectly and forever satisfies the law, namely, Christ's righteousness *(2 Cor. 5:21; Rom. 4:6-8)*.

"The sole condition on which this righteousness is credited to the believer is faith in the Lord Jesus Christ. Faith is called a 'condition,' not because it possesses any merit but because it is the only instrument

by which the soul apprehends Christ and
His righteousness."

Rom. 1:17; 3:25,26; 4:20,22;
Phil. 3:8-11; Gal. 2:16[1]

When I read the definition of justification, I was
amazed at what Jesus had really accomplished for you
and me. When we put our faith in Jesus, the Father
justified us. Even though we are guilty of many sins, He
judged us as perfectly obedient to the law.

He gave us the perfect righteousness of Jesus. He
declared us to be entitled to all the rewards arising from
perfect obedience to the law even though we didn't
deserve it. Justified means it is just as if we've done
everything right in the sight of God. Jesus took the
judgment we deserved, and we got the judgment that
Jesus deserves. That's amazing love!

When I was a teenager, I got pregnant before I was
married. I was a Christian girl, and I knew it was wrong.
The devil began to speak his lies to my heart:

*Your marriage will never be blessed because of
your sin.*

You have to pay for your sin for the rest of your life.

God is disappointed in you.

---

[1] Easton, Matthew George. Entry for 'Justification.' *Easton's Bible Dictionary*.
<http://www.studylight.org/dic/ebd/view.cgi?number=T2147>. 1897.

Because I believed the devil's lies, I lived condemned by my sin. I had a difficult marriage and felt like it was the punishment that I deserved.

Yet, in my journey to discovering who I am in Jesus, one day the Holy Spirit revealed to me that I am justified. When I sat in the courtroom and was being accused by the devil for my great sin, Jesus was my defense attorney (1 John 2:1,2.) He said, "Father, I took the punishment for all her sins. I gave her My perfect righteousness. She is free to be blessed as though she obeyed the law perfectly."

My heavenly Father who sat in the judge's seat slammed His gavel on the desk and said, "I don't remember a sin she has ever committed. She's entitled to all the advantages and rewards arising from perfect obedience to the law. She is justified because of her faith in My Son, Jesus."

I was free from the curse that was due to me based on the law. Jesus had set me free. I was justified. It was just as if I had never sinned. The question was, who was I going to agree with: the prosecuting attorney (the devil) or my defense attorney, Jesus Christ, who already paid for my freedom? I chose to believe in Jesus.

When I began to see myself as righteous and justified, I asked for God's grace in my marriage. The power of the Holy Spirit healed my heart and God's blessing began to come on our relationship. Today, my husband and I love each other very much, and our marriage is blessed because I am justified in Jesus.

Is there a sin in your past that you feel you have to pay for? Has the devil been speaking his lies to your heart? You can be free by receiving the gift of justification today.

Agree with what Jesus did for you and live free from all guilt and shame. Speak the truth out loud:

- Jesus took the punishment for all my sins. He freed me from all guilt and shame.
- My heavenly Father judges me perfectly righteous in Jesus.
- He declared me entitled to all the blessings rising from perfect obedience to the law because I am justified in Christ.

Prayer

Heavenly Father, thank You for justifying me in the court of law. I know I don't deserve the blessing for perfect obedience, but Jesus paid the price for me to be declared perfect in Your sight. Thank You for setting me free from all my past mistakes and giving me a new life. I am justified because of Jesus.

Day 4

I Am Free From Condemnation

Therefore, [there is] now no condemnation
(no adjudging guilty of wrong) for those
who are in Christ Jesus.

Romans 8:1 AMP

Jesus has given us the gift of no condemnation, yet many Christians still live under condemnation because they view themselves outside of Christ. They are still trying to be righteous through their human efforts instead of resting in the truth that Jesus has already made them righteous in Him.

Condemnation is feeling bad about yourself. It's a feeling of guilt for not quite measuring up. Anytime you have a negative view of yourself or you think God has a negative view of you, you're living in condemnation. Condemnation is a deception of the devil. He tries to make you feel guilty for everything. As a spouse, parent, friend, employee, or Christian, he's always trying to speak this lie to your heart, *You don't measure up.*

In John 8:1-11 NIV, Jesus shows us His heart toward those who have sinned in the story of the Pharisees bringing an adulterous woman before Jesus to be judged.

"Teacher, this woman was caught in the act of adultery. In the Law Moses commanded us to stone such women. Now what do you say?" (v. 4,5).

Jesus answered, "If any one of you is without sin, let him be the first to throw a stone at her" (v. 7).

After everyone had dropped their stones and walked away, Jesus looked at the woman with love in His eyes and said to her, "Woman, where are they? Has no one condemned you?" (v. 10).

She answered, "No one, sir" (v. 11).

And Jesus said, "Then neither do I condemn you.... Go now and leave your life of sin" (v. 11).

The law made it clear that this woman deserved punishment. She was judged guilty in the court of law, but Jesus in His great love set the woman free. He told her that He didn't judge her guilty of wrong.

Have we fully comprehended the amazing love our Savior has toward us? We all know in the Old Covenant that there were many instances where people were condemned and punished for their sins. We often hold on to that view of ourselves and God, but the truth is that our heavenly Father had a plan to release us from all guilt and condemnation by sending His Son, Jesus, to set us free.

> **Brothers, listen! We are here to proclaim that through this man Jesus there is forgiveness for your sins. Everyone who believes in him is declared right with God—something the law of Moses could never do.**
>
> *Acts 13:38,39* NLT

One time right before I was getting ready to teach a Bible study, I got very upset because of a disagreement I had with my husband. I remember as soon I as walked out of the room, the devil came immediately to condemn me. He held the law over my head and began accusing me with it. *You don't deserve to teach Bible study. Look at you, you just sinned.* I wanted to crawl in a hole and cry as condemnation began to envelop me. But instead I turned my thoughts toward Jesus and asked Him to help me. My Savior reminded me of a very powerful truth in the Bible.

> **God made you alive with Christ, for he forgave all our sins. He canceled the**

record of the charges against us and took it away by nailing it to the cross. In this way, he disarmed the spiritual rulers and authorities. He shamed them publicly by his victory over them on the cross. So don't let anyone condemn you.

Colossians 2:13-16 NLT

Jesus reminded me that He cancelled the charges against me by nailing them to the cross. The devil couldn't use the law to accuse me anymore. His weapon had been disarmed. The devil was the one who was shamed when Jesus won the victory for me. I didn't have to feel condemned anymore. I could receive His forgiveness and walk free. I remember how empowered I felt that day after the Holy Spirit had reminded me that there is no condemnation to those who are in Christ Jesus. I went to that Bible study and shared my recent revelation with every lady who was there, and they were also set free by the truth.

Jesus has forgiven all our sins. When He died on the cross, He paid the price for all of them to be cleared from our record. In Hebrews 8:12 NLT our heavenly Father says,

"I will forgive their wickedness, and I will never again remember their sins."

When the Father looks at us, He declares us innocent, perfect, and faultless because of Jesus.

The next time the devil tries to accuse and condemn you with the law, remember that Jesus looks at you with love in His eyes and says, "I do not condemn you, go and sin no more." So agree with the One who loves you. Speak the truth out loud:

- The charges that the devil uses to accuse me have been nailed to the cross.
- I am forgiven. I am free from all guilt and declared righteous.
- I am free from condemnation because of Jesus.

Prayer

Heavenly Father, thank You for reminding me that I am free from condemnation because I am in Christ. I don't have to feel guilty or condemned. You have forgiven me for all my wrongs, and You don't even remember one sin I've ever done.

I am truly free from all guilt because of Jesus.

Day 5

I Am Free From Sin

Our old sinful selves were crucified with Christ so that sin might lose its power in our lives. We are no longer slaves to sin. For when we died with Christ we were set free from the power of sin. Sin is no longer your master, for you no longer live under the requirements of the law. Instead, you live under the freedom of God's grace.

Romans 6:6–7,14 NLT

Your old sinful nature died on the cross with Jesus. You have a new nature of righteousness. Sin no longer has a hold on you. Jesus set you free from the Old Covenant, which was based on the law, and He brought you into the New Covenant of grace. The law simply reminds you of how guilty you are, but grace empowers you with God's ability to live free from all sin.

Have you ever had an area of your life you felt like you couldn't get victory over? I used to relate to the apostle Paul when he wrote in *Romans 7:18–19,24–25 NLT:*

> **And I know that nothing good lives in me, that is, in my sinful nature. I want to do what is right, but I can't. I want to do what is good, but I don't. I don't want to do what is wrong, but I do it anyway.**

> **Oh what a miserable person I am! Who will free me from this life that is dominated by sin and death? Thank God! The answer is in Jesus Christ our Lord.**

The devil would like you to believe the lie that you have to try harder, discipline yourself, or he may have even convinced you that you'll never change.

I remember as a young wife feeling so defeated. I seemed to always get into strife with my husband. Even though the Bible taught me to respect and honor him, instead I found myself being resentful and angry toward him. The law constantly condemned me.

One day I cried out to the Lord to show me the truth that would set me free. When I understood that Jesus had made me a righteous and godly wife, I began to see myself differently. When I was tempted to get angry or upset, I would run to Jesus and receive His grace to overcome.

> **For we do not have a high priest who is unable to sympathize with our weaknesses, but we have one who has been tempted in every way, just as we are—yet was without sin. Let us then approach the throne of grace with confidence, so that we may receive mercy and find grace to help us in our time of need.**
>
> *Hebrews 4:15,16 NIV*

I didn't have to depend on my own strength anymore. I could look to Jesus and trust Him to do the work in me.

> **[Not in your own strength] for it is God Who is all the while effectually at work in you [energizing and creating in you the power and desire], both to will and to work for His good pleasure and satisfaction and delight.**
>
> *Philippians 2:13 AMP*

I began to pray, "Lord create in me the desire and power to love my husband with your love." I want to act like You, Jesus, but I know I can't do it in my own strength."

His promise became the anchor of my soul as I looked to Jesus continually to transform me into His image. The more I saw myself as already righteous in Jesus and looked to Him daily for the grace I needed, the more I saw the fruit of righteousness come out in my life.

> **For the sin of this one man, Adam, caused death to rule over many. But even greater is God's wonderful grace and his gift of righteousness, for all who receive it will live in triumph over sin and death through this one man, Jesus Christ.**
>
> *Romans 5:17 NLT*

I have a friend who struggled with her weight her entire life. She was more than 100 pounds overweight and felt very condemned by it. She had tried for years to lose weight in her own strength. She would lose weight for a time but would simply gain it all back. She saw herself as a failure in this area of her life.

Then she began to believe who she was in Jesus. She began to see herself as a healthy righteous woman in

Christ. She asked Jesus daily to create in her the desire and power to exercise and eat healthy. We all watched as she was transformed from the inside out. Sin no longer had dominion over her. She triumphed over sin and death by receiving the gift of righteousness and His overflowing grace.

When you try to live by the law, it will only condemn you and keep you in the vicious cycle of sin, but when you truly begin to walk free from condemnation by seeing yourself as already righteous, already free in Jesus, sin will no longer have dominion over you. As you depend on Jesus to strengthen you, you'll live free from all sin.

So believe who you are in Jesus. Speak the truth out loud:

- I am free from the power of sin because of Jesus.
- I am the righteousness of God in Christ.
- God's grace empowers me to live free from sin.

Prayer

Heavenly Father, thank You for setting me free from the power of sin. When I am tempted, help me to remember who I am in You. I can run to Your throne of grace to receive the strength I need to overcome. Create in me the desire and power to bear the fruit of righteousness. I want my life to glorify You.

Day 6

I Am Valuable

For we are God's masterpiece. He has created us anew in Christ Jesus.
Ephesians 2:10 NLT

A masterpiece is a valuable work of art created by an artist. The word *valuable* means expensive, precious, priceless, and important. You're valuable, precious, and important because God created you as a new person in Jesus. You're His masterpiece.

Yet, there are many people who don't believe they are valuable because they seek their worth from something other than their relationship with Jesus. When a person bases their value on the world's system, it often leads to low self-esteem and self-worth.

Have you ever compared yourself to others and based your value on…

- …how you look?
- …how many friends you have?
- …what others think of you?
- …how much you do to help someone?
- …your social status?
- …how well you do something?
- …your job or position?
- …how much you're needed?

When we base our value on these things, we fall into the trap of the enemy. We begin to believe that we're not needed; we're not important or valuable.

I used to base my value on how I compared to others. I thought, *She's better then me. She has a better personality than I do. They like her more than me. She's prettier, smarter, and more gifted then I am.* All of these comparisons made me think less of myself. They made me feel less valuable and important. Sometimes I would focus on something that I was better at just to make myself feel better, but deep down I didn't believe I measured up. Have you ever compared yourself to others and felt this way?

The value of something is determined by what someone is willing to pay for it. Let's look at how much Jesus was willing to pay for you and me.

You know that God paid a ransom to save you from the empty life you inherited from your ancestors. And the ransom He paid was not mere gold or silver. It was the precious blood of Christ, the sinless, spotless, Lamb of God.

1 Peter 1:18,19 NLT

When I realized that Jesus proved His love for me by purchasing me with His precious blood, I began to see myself as valuable. I don't have to compare myself to others anymore or look to them to find my value. I can believe the truth that I am valuable and important not based on what I do or how well I perform or how I compare to others. I am valuable because Jesus paid a great price for me. I don't have to base my value on the world's system. I can live in God's kingdom and allow the truth of what Jesus did for me to define how valuable and important I am.

I have two daughters who are still at home, and I have two grown sons. The Lord has also blessed me with a beautiful daughter-in-law and a granddaughter. They have all been such a joy in my life. All I have ever wanted to be is a wife and mother. To this day when someone asks me what I do, my first response is, "I'm a mom."

Not too long ago, my heart was feeling sad because my boys had grown up, and I didn't feel like they needed me anymore. I remember taking my heart to Jesus and talking to Him about how I was feeling. He began to show me that I was looking to my boys needing me to find value and worth in this world. He reminded me that I am valuable because of the price He paid for me. My value is found in who I am in Jesus.

Have you found yourself looking to something else besides Jesus to determine your value? I encourage you today to let Jesus define how valuable you are. Your value is not found in how you compare to others, how well you do something or a position that you hold, it is found in who you are in Jesus. So believe who you are in Him and speak the truth out loud:

- I am a masterpiece because the Master created me.
- I am precious and important in Jesus.
- I am valuable because of the great price Jesus paid for me.

Prayer

Heavenly Father, thank You for showing me how valuable, precious, and important I am to You. Jesus paid a great price for me. I don't have to look anywhere else to find my value. I can be happy and secure in the truth that I am valuable because I am Your masterpiece. Thank You for loving me so much.

Day 7

I Am Special

But you are a chosen race, a royal priesthood, a dedicated nation, [God's] own purchased, special people.

1 Peter 2:9 AMP

You are God's treasured possession. He purchased you with the precious blood of Jesus. You are His special purchased daughter. *Special* means to pay close attention to, unique, and treasured. When someone celebrates your birthday, it makes you feel special because you get all the attention. All of heaven celebrated the day you became a part of God's family.

When I was a young girl, I didn't feel very special. My younger brother, the baby of the family, got a lot of attention. My older sister always seemed to get praised

for how good she was. The devil would constantly speak
these lies to my heart:

You don't even belong to this family.

You're not special.

Nobody pays attention to you.

Your sister is better than you.

Your parents love them more than they love you.

These lies that I believed created brokenness in my heart.

It wasn't until I was an adult that I began to understand the truth that healed my heart and set me free.
When I learned how important I was to Jesus, I began
to feel very special. Jesus said:

> **Not a single sparrow can fall to the ground
> without your Father knowing it. And the
> very hairs of your head are all numbered.
> So don't be afraid; you are more valuable
> to God than a whole flock of sparrows**
>
> *Matthew 10:29-31* NLT

I realized from this scripture that my heavenly
Father pays very special attention to me. If He knows
me so well and watches over me so closely that He
knows how many hairs are on my head, I must be very
special to Him.

You watched me as I was being formed in utter seclusion, as I was woven together in the dark of the womb. You saw me before I was born. Every day of my life was recorded in your book. Every moment was laid out before a single day had passed. How precious are your thoughts about me, O God. They cannot be numbered! I can't even count them; they outnumber the grains of sand! And when I wake up, you are still with me!

Psalm 139:15-18 NLT

As you were being formed in your mother's womb, your heavenly Father was watching you. He delighted in you and wrote down in His book the specific plan and purpose He had for your life. He had it all planned out before you even took your first breath. You're an important part of His plan. His thoughts toward you are precious. You can't even count how many loving thoughts He has toward you each day.

When I began to believe this truth, I began to feel important. The truth is that we are so special to our heavenly Father that He pays extra close attention to us. Jesus was God's special Son, but when Jesus came to live inside of you and me, we became His special ones too. In

John 17:23 NIV Jesus is talking to the Father and He says, "You…have loved them even as you have loved me." God loves you just as much as He loves Jesus. He doesn't see any of us as more important or more special than the others. He loves us all the same. You're very special and treasured by your heavenly Father. There is no one else just like you. He has given you His full attention because He wants you to feel very loved.

So the next time the devil attempts to deceive you with his lies, remember who you are in Jesus and agree with the One who loves you. Speak the truth out loud:

- I am my Father's purchased, special daughter.
- He pays special attention to me. He never leaves me.
- He wrote down His special plan for my life before I was ever born.

Prayer

Heavenly Father, thank You for showing me how special I am to You. You purchased me with the precious blood of Jesus. I am your special child, and You pay such close attention to me that You even know how many hairs are on my head. You even wrote down Your unique plan for my life before I was born. Your thoughts about me are precious, and that makes me feel so loved.

Day 8

I Am Accepted

He hath made us accepted in the beloved.
Ephesians 1:6

Your heavenly Father accepts you because of your faith in Jesus. The word *accepted* means chosen, approved, and favored. When someone accepts you, it means that they want you to be a part of their life. They want to be your friend. They approve of you.

God put a need within your heart to feel accepted. Yet, we often look to other people to meet that need, and we end up feeling rejected. Rejection is something we've all faced at one time or another. It may have been a boyfriend, an employer, or maybe even a spouse, child, or a parent. Abandonment and divorce can cause you to have a negative view of yourself, and they paint a picture on your heart that says, "Rejected."

The devil uses these opportunities to try and get you to believe his lies. He throws fiery darts at your heart that say:

You're not good enough.

They don't like you.

You're rejected.

From the time I was a young girl growing up in school to the present, I have experienced rejection in my life. I have had boys reject me, friends turn their backs on me, and people say mean things about me. We have all experienced these types of rejection in our lives.

I used to look to people to find acceptance. Their opinion of me affected my heart in a deep way. I found myself concerned about whether they would accept me and want to be my friend. I worried about what they thought of me. The fear of rejection is something we've all faced. It causes us to pull away from relationships with others to protect ourselves. Fear of rejection is a life of bondage, but Jesus came to set us free.

We can rejoice in our wonderful new relationship with God because our Lord Jesus Christ has made us friends of God.... Even greater is God's wonderful grace and his gift of forgiveness to many through this other man, Jesus Christ. And the result of

God's gracious gift is very different from the result of that one man's sin. For Adam's sin led to condemnation, but God's free gift leads to our being made right with God, even though we are guilty of many sins.

Romans 5:11,15–16 NLT

The good news is that Jesus gave you and me the gift of forgiveness so that we could be fully accepted by our heavenly Father. The result of Adam's sin caused us all to be rejected, but Jesus' free gift of righteousness led us to being accepted forever. People often accept or reject us based on our actions, but the Bible says even though we are guilty of many sins, Jesus has given us the gracious gift of complete acceptance.

Jesus wants you to have godly friends, but He wants to be your best friend forever. He'll never reject you, never turn His back on you, and never talk bad about you. You can share your heart with Him, and He'll always love and accept you no matter what you say or do. He's the kind of best friend we're all searching for.

When you believe what Jesus says about you, you'll live free from the fear of rejection. You'll be completely confident in the truth that you are accepted by the most important One in the whole world, your heavenly

Father, the King of kings. You are royalty. You can be friendly to those around you, and if they don't like you, that's okay because Jesus has met the need within your heart to feel accepted. You can be confident in His great love.

So the next time you are feeling rejected by someone, don't let him or her define who you are. Turn your thoughts to Jesus and remember who you are in Him. Agree with the One who loves you. Speak the truth out loud:

- Because of Jesus, I am good enough.
- Jesus is my best friend.
- I am loved and accepted by Him.

Prayer

Heavenly Father, thank You for loving and accepting me. Help me to believe who I am in Jesus. I don't ever have to fear being rejected because I am completely accepted in Jesus. When I believe the truth, it makes my heart happy, and I am able to love others with Your love. Thank You, Jesus, for being my best friend forever.

Day 9

I Am Chosen

**Even before he made the world, God loved
us and chose us in Christ to be holy and
without fault in his eyes.**

Ephesians 1:4 NLT

Even before God made the world, He loved you and
chose you to belong to Him. Before you were even born,
you were a part of His plan. He invited you to be a part
of His family. When you accepted His invitation, you
became one with Jesus. Now your heavenly Father sees
you as holy and perfect in Christ. You are without fault
in His eyes because of Jesus. Jesus met the need within
your heart to be loved and chosen.

Yet, when we look outside of Jesus to meet this need
within our heart, we often become disappointed. There
are times when we have all felt like we didn't belong.

Have you ever wanted to be a part of a group of people but felt like they really didn't want you? I know there have been times in my life when I felt this way.

I remember a time when I was talking to someone, and she was telling me that she was getting together with a group of people. I wondered why I hadn't been invited to join them. The devil uses these opportunities to tempt us to believe his lies. He doesn't want us to believe the truth, so He plants these negative thoughts in our minds:

You're not wanted.

There's something wrong with you.

You don't belong.

We all want to be chosen by someone. We want people to like us in order to have a sense of belonging. It's interesting to note that in the world's system, whether it's an employee, a spouse, or a friend, people look for certain criteria before they choose the people they want to be a part of their life. For example, when you apply for a job, if you don't meet the qualifications for that position or if someone else is more qualified than you, you aren't the one chosen. If you don't know who you are in Jesus, this would reinforce the lie that there's something wrong with you.

When we look to our parents, spouse, children, employer, church leader, or friend to make us feel wanted and chosen, our self-image is distorted. We end up believing the enemy's lies over the truth of who we are in Jesus.

The good news is that when we look to Jesus, we'll never be disappointed. He has chosen you to be a part of His royal family. You belong to the most important family in the whole world. Your heavenly Father is the King of kings. When He looks at you, you meet all the criteria because in Jesus you are without fault and perfect in His sight. He chose you before the foundations of the world. Your name was on His invitation list. He didn't forget you.

He didn't choose you because you were good at something or because you performed well. He chose you just because He loves you. He picked you so you would believe that you were special. Jesus speaks His words of love to our hearts and says, "I want you because I chose you to belong to Me. You are perfect in My sight."

When you believe the truth, it doesn't matter anymore if someone chooses you or not. You have already been chosen by Jesus, the King of kings:

> **You didn't choose me. I chose you.**
> *John 15:16 NLT*

So the next time the devil throws a fiery dart at your heart and tells you that nobody wants you or you don't belong, look to Jesus and let Him fill your heart with the truth of His love. Remember who you are in Him and speak the truth out loud:

- My heavenly Father invited me to belong to His royal family.
- He sees me as perfect and without fault because of Jesus.
- I am loved and chosen by the King of kings.

Prayer

Heavenly Father, thank You for choosing me to be a part of Your royal family. I now know when the devil tries to lie to me and tell me that I don't belong and nobody wants me, that it's not true. I belong to You. You chose me in Christ before the foundation of the world to be holy and without fault in Your eyes. Help me to remember who I am in Jesus. I am chosen and loved by You.

Day 10

I Am Approved

Before I formed you in the womb I knew [and] approved of you.

Jeremiah 1:5 AMP

Before you were ever born, before you were able to do anything right or wrong, your heavenly Father approved of you. *Approve* means to have or express a favorable opinion of someone and to be very pleased with them. When your heavenly Father thinks of you, He smiles. He always has a good opinion of you. He's pleased with you not because you've done everything right but because you believe in Jesus.

Have you ever worried about someone's opinion of you? Have you ever tried to gain someone's approval? We all seek approval and want others to be pleased with us. Yet, we've all experienced a time when we did something wrong and it caused someone to look at us with disapproval. That look that we're all familiar with caused us to think, *They're not happy with me. I've done something to make them mad.*

You may also think that when you do something wrong, God is angry and disapproves of you. The devil wants to separate you from your heavenly Father. He wants you to feel bad about yourself, so he speaks these lies to your heart:

God is angry at you.

He doesn't approve of you because of your bad behavior.

He is not pleased with you.

Through a story in the Bible, Jesus showed us how the Father looks at us when we do wrong. In Luke 15:11-24 NIV, Jesus tells a story of a father of two sons. The father gave one of his sons a lot of money, but the son was foolish with it and wasted it on a sinful lifestyle. His bad behavior brought much sadness into his life and he found himself poor, sad, and rejected by everyone.

When the son ran out of money and friends, he remembered how the servants were even treated well in his father's home; so he decided to go back to his father and say, "I am no longer worthy to be called your son; make me like one of your hired men" (v. 19).

He thought his father might be angry with him and reject him because of his bad behavior. But when the father saw his son walking toward him, he was so happy that he ran, embraced him, and kissed his face. The father's heart was filled with love and compassion toward his son.

Then the son began to say, "Father, I have sinned against heaven and against you. I am no longer worthy to be called your son" (v. 21).

His father replied, "Quick! Bring the best robe and put it on him. Put a ring on his finger and sandals on his feet. Bring the fattened calf and kill it. Let's have a feast and celebrate. For this son of mine was dead and is alive again; he was lost and is found" (vv. 22-24).

Jesus told this story so you could understand how your heavenly Father feels toward you when you've done wrong. When He looks at you, His heart is filled with love and compassion. He doesn't want you to sin because He knows that it will bring sadness into your life, but it doesn't change the way He feels about you. He'll always love and approve of you. Listen to His promise to you:

> **"Just as I swore in the time of Noah that I would never again let a flood cover the earth, so now I swear that I will never again be angry and punish you. For**

the mountains may move and the hills disappear, but even then my faithful love for you will remain. My covenant of blessing will never be broken," says the LORD, who has mercy on you.

Isaiah 54:9,10 NLT

The truth is, because you believe in Jesus, you'll always have your heavenly Father's approval. He'll never change His good opinion of you. He promises that He'll never be angry with you or tell you that you're bad. When you believe who you are in Jesus, you don't have to look to others anymore to feel approved.

In John 5:41 NLT, Jesus is talking to some people and He says, "Your approval means nothing to me." He didn't need the approval of men because He had the approval of His Father.

So the next time you feel like someone is disapproving of you, look to Jesus and remember who you are in Him. Speak the truth out loud:

- My heavenly Father will never be angry with me.
- He approves of me because of Jesus.
- I'm His beloved daughter, and He is pleased with me because I believe in Jesus.

Prayer

Heavenly Father, thank You for forgiving me when I do wrong. I now know that You'll never be angry at me. I have Your approval because Jesus took away all my sins and made me perfect in Your sight. You're pleased with me because I believe in Jesus. I feel so happy to be loved by You!

Day 11

I Am Wonderfully Made

I praise you because I am fearfully and wonderfully made; your works are wonderful, I know that full well.

Psalm 139:14 NIV

God made you wonderful. The word *wonderful* means "amazing, astonishing, incredible, worthy of admiration, and marvelous"[2] This is who you are in Jesus and what your heavenly Father thinks of you.

It's important to God that you see yourself the way He sees you. He knew there would be times that you wouldn't think you were wonderful because someone told you that you were bad or because you did something wrong that made you feel bad about yourself.

---

[2] Charlton Laird, Webster's New World Thesaurus, (New York, NY: Simon & Shuster Adult Publishing Group, 2003), s.v. "wonderful."

The devil's goal is to make you believe the opposite of what Jesus says about you. He wants you to believe the lie that you're not wonderful. So the next time you have negative feelings about yourself, you can know that it's the enemy working on your heart to try and get you to believe his lies.

I had a friend who got really upset with me one time because of something I had said. It was a miscommunication: she misunderstood what I had meant. The next time she saw me, she proceeded to tell me how horrible I was. She told me my heart was wrong and that it might be better if I just left and never came back. Her words cut to my heart like a knife. I couldn't believe she was saying such judgmental and critical things about me. I thought she was my friend. As tears rolled down my face, I told her I was sorry for anything I may have said that hurt her, but it didn't change the way she felt about me. I left our conversation feeling bad. I knew in my heart that the things she said about me weren't true, but I hated the idea that she thought that way about me.

As I took my heart to Jesus, He reminded me that He thought I was wonderful. As I thought about His precious thoughts about me, His love began to heal my broken heart. I began to feel compassion rise up for my friend, and the hurt I felt began to melt away.

The truth is that no matter what anyone else thinks, our heavenly Father always thinks we're wonderful because of Jesus.

> **How precious are your thoughts about me, O God. They cannot be numbered! I can't even count them; they outnumber the grains of sand!**
> *Psalm 139:17,18 NLT*

It is pretty amazing to think that out of all the billions of people in the world, you can't even count how many precious thoughts the Father thinks toward you every day. His thoughts toward you are precious. He thinks you're excellent, marvelous, amazing, and exceptionally outstanding. He made you wonderful.

Have you ever watched the popular television show American Idol™? On this program, contestants are judged by how well they sing a song. They are trying to earn the good opinion of the people by how well they perform. They want everyone to think they are wonderful and amazing. Have you ever wished that people would think of you like that?

God has put this need in all of us, and the good news is that no matter how well you perform, His opinion of you never changes. He always thinks you're wonderful because of Jesus. You're a daughter of the King, and He loves you very much. Nothing you do will ever change His love for you. What your heavenly Father says about you is true.

So if someone has a bad opinion of you, turn your heart to Jesus and remember who you are in Him. Agree with the One who loves you. Speak the truth out loud:

- Jesus made me wonderful.
- He thinks I am marvelous, excellent, and amazing.
- I am significant because of Jesus.

Prayer

Heavenly Father, You created me, and I am wonderfully made. Your thoughts toward me are precious. I can't even count how many loving thoughts You have about me each day. Help me not to worry about what others think but to keep my mind on Your precious thoughts about me. You made me wonderful, marvelous, and amazing. Thank You, Father, for loving me with Your unconditional love.

Day 12

I Am Adored

The Lord your God is in the midst of you, a Mighty One, a Savior [Who saves]! He will rejoice over you with joy; He will rest [in silent satisfaction] and in His love He will be silent and make no mention [of past sins, or even recall them]; He will exult over you with singing.

***Zephaniah 3:17** AMP*

I remember growing up in church singing a song to Jesus that went like this: "I exult you; I exult you; I exult you; oh, Lord" We would sing to the Lord every Sunday, lifting Him up in adoration. One day as I was reading Zephaniah 3:17, I realized that Jesus exults over you and me with singing too! *Exult* means to leap for joy, to be extremely joyful, and to delight in.

I'm sure you've seen fans of a movie star or a popular music group leaping for joy at the sight of the one they adore. Well, just imagine, Jesus, the King of kings, adoring you in that way. He exults over you. He is singing songs of love over you to let you know how very much you delight His heart. He adores you.

Your enemy, the devil, doesn't want you to believe that anyone adores you. He wants to fill your head with this lie, *How can God adore you when you've made so many mistakes?* But the good news is that your heavenly Father doesn't even remember one thing you've ever done wrong. You stand clean and holy before Him because of the blood of Jesus. Zephaniah 3:17 says that in God's love, He makes no mention of your past sins nor does He even recall them. Jesus has set you free from all of your mistakes. Jude 1:24 AMP says,

> **Now to Him Who is able to keep you without stumbling or slipping or falling, and to present [you] unblemished (blameless and faultless) before the presence of His glory in triumphant joy and exultation [with unspeakable, ecstatic delight].**

Wow! Think about that for a minute. Jesus presents you blameless and without a single fault before the

Father. The emotion that He feels when He looks at you is triumphant joy and exultation and ecstatic delight.

In March of 2008, I became a new grandma. When my granddaughter was about three months old, I sat out on my back porch and rocked her to sleep in my arms. As I looked at her beautiful face, I felt a deep love in my heart. She was so innocent and pure. She was perfect in my eyes, and I began to sing this song over her from my heart:

Jesus loves Ryann and grandma does too.

We think she's wonderful, yes we do!

Precious and sweet and beautiful too.

We love Ryann, yes, we do!

Over and over again I sang this song out of my adoration for her. I remember singing songs of love over my own children when they were babies. Over and over again I would sing about how wonderful they were. These memories make me smile.

As I sat and delighted in my new sweet grandbaby and thanked God for her, I heard my heavenly Father whisper to my heart, "That's the way I feel about you," and He reminded me of Zephaniah 3:17. All of the sudden that verse took on a whole new meaning. I understood it in a deeper way. I sat there in silence as I listened to my heavenly Father sing a love song over me. He adores me, just as I adore Ryann.

Have you ever sung over one of your children or grandchildren, or have you looked at them with love and adoration? That's the way your heavenly Father sings over you. He loves you more than you could ever imagine. He delights in you. He thinks you are perfect. You make Him smile.

As you go about your day, remember that your heavenly Father is so happy you are His that He exults over you with singing. He adores you!

Realizing how the Father rejoices over you gives you a security that no one else can give or take away. On your journey to discovering who you are in Jesus, speak the truth out loud and fill your heart with His love:

- My heavenly Father is singing with joy over me. He delights in me.
- I am without fault in His sight because of Jesus.
- He adores me.

Prayer

Heavenly Father, my heart is changed by the way You love and adore me. Help me to see You dancing and singing over me because I am Your beloved child. When I begin to feel bad about myself, help me remember how You feel about me. Thank You for loving me so much.

Day 13

I Am Seated in Christ

And He raised us up together with Him and made us sit down together [giving us joint seating with Him] in the heavenly sphere [by virtue of our being] in Christ Jesus.

Ephesians 2:6 AMP

In our world people are constantly seeking positions of honor and power. Something in our human nature wants to be honored and praised. We want the best position, the one that validates and make us feel the most valuable. There is no greater or higher position than to be seated next to the King of kings, the Father, God, in His kingdom. Jesus earned this place of honor.

> Because of the joy awaiting him, he
> endured the cross, disregarding its shame.
> Now he is seated in the place of honor
> beside God's throne.
>
> *Hebrews 12:2 NLT*

In Mark 10:35-40 AMP, we read a story of two disciples named James and John who came to Jesus with a request: "And they said to Him, Grant that we may sit, one at Your right hand and one at [Your] left hand, in Your glory (Your majesty and splendor)" (v. 37).

Then Jesus replied, "To sit at My right hand or at My left hand is not Mine to give; but [it will be given to those] for whom it is ordained and prepared" (v. 40).

James and John knew that the highest place of honor would be to sit next to Jesus in His glory. When the other disciples heard that the brothers had asked for this position, they were angered by it. Everyone wanted such a place of recognition and importance. Isn't it typical that jealousy and anger is the result of people fighting for a position?

What the disciples didn't realize was that our heavenly Father wasn't going to give anyone a position next to Jesus. He was going to give every one of His children the very seat of Jesus. He raised us up together with Him and made us sit down together, giving us joint seating with Him. He placed us in the seat of highest honor in Christ Jesus. You have the highest position in the universe. There is no greater place of power or honor than the place where Jesus sits next to the Father.

The devil doesn't want us to know that we sit in such a high place of honor. He wants us to continue to struggle and strive for an important earthly position. He wants us to seek the praise and honor that comes from man because he knows that it will never satisfy our soul. Jesus said in John 5:44 AMP:

> **How is it possible for you to believe [how can you learn to believe], you who [are content to seek and] receive praise and honor and glory from one another, and yet do not seek the praise and honor and glory which come from Him Who alone is God?**

Jesus' point was that you will never truly be free as long as what others think of you is more important than what the Father thinks of you. If you keep striving to obtain man's approval and praise, you'll never find true peace and security in this world. Give up seeking man's praise and honor and rest in the honor and praise that your heavenly Father has freely poured out upon you in Jesus.

Everyday He honors you by acknowledging the truth that you are royalty, righteous, justified, valuable, special, accepted, chosen, approved, wonderful, and adored because you are in Christ Jesus. When you accept this truth, you will rest knowing that no earthly position could ever compare to the place where you already sit in Christ. The King of kings honors and esteems you before all of heaven. You are true royalty in the kingdom of God.

So the next time the enemy tries to tempt you to seek after a position so that you might receive the praise and honor of man, remember who you are in Jesus, and speak the truth out loud:

- I am seated in Christ in the highest place of honor.
- My heavenly Father honors me by reminding me of who I am in Jesus.
- I am validated in Christ Jesus.

Prayer

Heavenly Father, thank You for showing me the truth of my position in Christ. I am seated in Jesus in the highest place of honor. I no longer need to strive for an earthly position to feel valuable. I don't have to seek the praise and honor that comes from men. I am seated in the highest position in the universe, and You honor me daily by reminding me of how special, valuable, and important I am. I can rest in Your great love for me.

Day 14

I Am a Joint Heir With Jesus

You have not received a spirit that makes
you fearful slaves. Instead, you received
God's Spirit when he adopted you as his
own children. Now we call him, "Abba,
Father." For his Spirit joins with our spirit
to affirm that we are God's children. And
since we are his children, we are his heirs.
In fact, together with Christ we are heirs
of God's glory.

Romans 8:15-17 NLT

How does a fearful slave act? A slave tries to earn
his master's approval through his performance. If he
works hard and does a good job, he is rewarded, but if he
fails to meet his master's expectations, he is punished. A
slave is fearful because he is never quite sure he is good
enough to receive his master's blessing.

For so long in my Christian life, I acted like a fearful slave when it came to my relationship with my heavenly Father. I tried really hard to be good enough to earn His promises in my life. I was often concerned that I hadn't done all that was needed to deserve His blessing. I was constantly striving to get it right.

I didn't know who I was because the enemy had deceived me with these lies:

You're not worthy of God's promises.
You have to do more to deserve His blessing.
God probably won't come through for you.

All of these lies I believed caused me to be fearful when I faced negative circumstances in my life. Worry, fear, and condemnation were the result of seeing myself as a slave instead of as a daughter of the King of kings.

When I realized that the enemy had deceived me into acting like a fearful slave, I asked my heavenly Father to show me the truth that would set me free. When I received the truth that I am a joint heir with Jesus and that God's promises are my inheritance in Christ, I entered into rest. I don't have to try to earn something that already belongs to me.

You are no longer a slave but God's own child. And since you are his child, God has made you his heir.

Galatians 4:7 NLT

You're no longer a slave to the law. You don't have to try to measure up in order to be worthy. You are a child of the King, a joint heir with Jesus to every one of God's promises. His righteousness, wisdom, guidance, power, provision, healing, deliverance, favor, and blessing are your inheritance in Christ. You don't have to try to earn it through obedience to the law. Jesus earned all of God's promises through His perfect obedience, and now that you are His bride, everything He earned He has given to you as a gift of grace. Everything He has belongs to you, and you can rest in Him.

> **For the Son of God, Jesus Christ, who was preached among you by me and Silas and Timothy, was not "Yes" and "No," but in him it has always been "Yes." For no matter how many promises God has made, they are "Yes" in Christ. And so through him the "Amen" is spoken by us to the glory of God.**
>
> *2 Corinthians 1:19,20 NIV*

God's answer is always "yes" whenever you ask Him to bring His promise to pass in your life because you are in Christ Jesus. He doesn't change His mind from day to day depending on your behavior. When you come boldly to the throne of grace and ask for whatever you need, your heavenly Father always says, "Yes, my child, everything I have belongs to you." So through Jesus, you can boldly say, "Amen," and agree with the One who loves you.

So the next time the devil tempts you to live like a fearful slave, remember who you are in Jesus. Speak the truth out loud:

- I am not a fearful slave. I am a child of God and a joint heir with Jesus.
- Everything my heavenly Father has belongs to me.
- God's promises are "yes" and "amen" in my life because I am in Christ Jesus.

Prayer

Thank You, heavenly Father, for adopting me as Your child. I don't have to live like a fearful slave by trying to earn Your approval and blessing. All of Your promises are "yes" in my life because I am in Christ Jesus. I am a joint heir with Jesus to all of Your promises. Everything You have belongs to me because I am Your beloved child. I can live confident and secure in Your unchanging love.

Day 15

I Am Favored

For surely, O LORD, you bless the righteous; you surround them with your favor as with a shield.

Psalm 5:12 NIV

Favor is part of your inheritance in Christ. *Favor* means a friendly regard shown toward another or a gracious act of kindness. When you believe who you are in Jesus, He'll cause others to look upon you favorably. He'll surround you with people who are friendly and generous toward you.

The devil doesn't want you to think you're favored, so he attempts to get you to believe these lies:

They're not going to like you.

You're not blessed.

It's not going to work out for you.

When we believe the lies of the enemy and someone does try to bless us, we have a hard time receiving it because down deep we don't think we deserve it. This is not how your Savior created you to live. He wants you to believe who you are in Him and enjoy His favor and blessing upon your life.

Last year I was looking for office space for Because of Jesus Ministries. I had prayed about it and asked the Lord to guide and direct me to the right place. I had called on a few places, but nothing felt right. I continued to thank the Lord for blessing me with favor and preparing a place for us to do the work of the ministry. One day I had a sweet friend of mine call to tell me that she knew a couple who was moving their business out of state, and they had some office space that would soon be available.

On my way to meeting with this couple, I thanked the Lord that if this was the office space He had for me, He would cause them to look upon me favorably. When I went to see the office, it was much bigger and more beautiful than I had pictured in my mind. As I walked around, I thought, *Heavenly Father, You're so good to me; Your blessing and favor surround me because of Jesus.* When I talked with the couple about moving into their space, they offered to give me one month of free rent, and they also donated a phone system and $21,000 worth of beautiful office furniture to the ministry. All we had to do was move in. God truly surrounded us with favor and blessed us far beyond what we had hoped for. Everywhere we go, we should believe that we are surrounded by favor because that is what Jesus promised.

Last year both my daughter-in-law and oldest son applied for promotions at their jobs. In both cases, there were others that had applied as well. We talked about how they didn't have to be worried about their interviews because they had the favor of God surrounding them. God would cause their employers to look upon them favorably. If it was God's plan for them, they'd get those positions, but if not, it just meant He had something better.

There is such peace in knowing that God loves you and that He is working out His plan for your life. Romans 8:28 says that He's working everything out for our good because He's called us to fulfill His purpose. His favor surrounds you wherever you go, and you can rest in who you are in Him. He will cause others to look favorably on you so that His plan will be accomplished in your life. Both my daughter-in-law and my son got the promotions, and they have been very blessed by them. God's blessing and favor continue to surround them like a shield.

And Jesus increased in wisdom…and in stature and years, and in favor with God and man.

Luke 2:52 AMP

Jesus lives inside of you. You are just like Him. You have favor with God and with man because of Jesus. As you look to Jesus and believe who you are in Him, you'll experience His favor upon your life.

When I think upon the truth that favor surrounds me like a shield, fear fades away and a quiet confidence resides in my soul. God didn't promise that everyone will like us, but He did say He would surround us with people who do. When we look to Him, He'll help us be confident and secure in His love. So believe who you are in Jesus, and speak the truth out loud:

- I am righteous in Jesus, and He surrounds me with favor as a shield.
- God will fulfill His purpose in my life.
- I have favor with God and man because of Jesus.

Prayer

Heavenly Father, thank You for surrounding me with favor. Help me to believe what You say about me and see myself as favored and blessed in You. I know You're working out Your plan for me. I trust You because I know You love me.

Day 16

I Am a Success

Give thanks to God! He always leads us in the winners' parade because we belong to Christ.

2 Corinthians 2:14 NIrV

Everyone wants to be a winner. You are a winner because you belong to Jesus. He defeated the enemy and his kingdom of darkness when He died on the cross for you and me. He rose again in triumphant victory, and He is the Winner. First John 4:17 says, "as he is, so are we in this world." Jesus leads you in the winners' parade because you are on His winning team. Nothing anyone says or nothing you do will ever change the truth that you are a winner because of Jesus.

Jesus made you a success. The question is, do you see yourself the way Jesus sees you? What you believe about yourself will make all the difference as to whether or not you experience the success that Jesus purchased for you.

The Bible says the devil is the accuser of the brethren, and he doesn't want you to succeed in life. He wants you to be full of fear and feel like a failure, so he tries to get you to believe his lies. Many times when I have attempted to do something that seemed difficult, I would hear these thoughts in my mind:

You can't do it.

What if you fail?

You're going to look like a failure.

These were all lies of the devil, and he was trying to paint a negative picture of me on my heart. He wanted me to believe the lie that I can't do it so that I would feel like a failure and quit.

Proverbs 23:7 NKJV says, "As he thinks in his heart, so is he." What we think about ourselves is what we'll experience in our lives. If we believe the lies of the devil, it will keep us in fear. When we do try to do something, fear will hinder us from doing our best. This confirms the lie that the devil has written on our heart that we're losers. Yet, Jesus already defeated the devil, and everything the devil says is a lie. Jesus is constantly speaking His words of love into our hearts. Jesus says that we can do all things through Him. (Phil. 4:13.) He made you a success. (2 Cor. 2:14.)

On the popular TV program American Idol™, twelve talented singers are performing in order to try and win the position of the next "American Idol." One day while I was watching, I heard the host ask one of the contestants if she thought she would win the competition. Her response was, "It doesn't matter whether I win or lose. I'm already a winner."

I remember thinking, *Wow, regardless of the outcome of the competition, she already sees herself as a winner.* She saw herself as a success. She performed with confidence because she was not afraid of losing. Regardless of what the judges said, this contestant had already decided in her heart that she was a winner. Not even the votes of the people could change that.

The same is true with you and me. One of the things that I was afraid to do was speak in front of people. Because of my fear, I would be nervous and not do as well as I wanted. Then I realized that Jesus had already made me a winner. I was a success because I belonged to Him. I began to think, *What do I have to lose if Jesus already made me a success?* No matter what people thought of me or how they might judge me, it would never change the truth that I am a success because of

Jesus. I became very confident about speaking in front of people because I believed who I am in Jesus.

The next time the devil tries to get you to quit by telling you that you can't do it, look to Jesus and remember who you are in Him. Success is part of your inheritance in Christ so speak the truth out loud:

- I can do all things through Christ.
- Jesus made me a success.
- I am a winner because of Jesus.

Prayer

Thank You, Jesus, for showing me that I'm a winner because I belong to You. I don't have to be afraid that I will fail because You've already made me a success. I can do all things through You. I am capable and successful in You!

Day 17

I Am Abundantly Blessed

For you are becoming progressively acquainted with and recognizing more strongly and clearly the grace of our Lord Jesus Christ (His kindness, His gracious generosity, His undeserved favor and spiritual blessing), [in] that though He was [so very] rich, yet for your sakes He became [so very] poor, in order that by His poverty you might become enriched (abundantly supplied).

2 Corinthians 8:9 AMP

Jesus took the curse of poverty and lack so that you might live in the blessing of abundance. Abundance is your inheritance as a child of God. You are a joint heir with Jesus. He is the God of more than enough. Yet, the enemy has tried to deceive many of God's children into believing these lies:

God wants you to be poor.

You're not blessed.

You're not going to have enough.

These lies create fear in our hearts and cause us to live far below the life Jesus came to give us.

The truth is that you are righteous in Jesus and His blessing is upon you, "Prosperity is the reward of the righteous" (Prov. 13:21 NIV). The Bible also says, "For You, Lord, will bless the [uncompromisingly] righteous" (Ps. 5:12 AMP).

The word *blessed* means that you are anointed and empowered to prosper. I love to think about how I am anointed and empowered to prosper because Jesus made me righteous. The Bible says that God takes care of the righteous in difficult times, "Even in famine they will have more than enough" (Ps. 37:19 NLT).

And God is able to make all grace (every favor and earthly blessing) come to you in abundance, so that you may always and under all circumstances and whatever the need be self-sufficient [possessing enough to require no aid or support and furnished

in abundance for every good work and charitable donation].

2 Corinthians 9:8 AMP

In 2001 the economy was declining and people were losing their jobs. It was a difficult time for a lot of people. My husband came home from work one day and told me he was going to lose his job as well. I remember the feeling of fear that tried to grip my heart. What were we going to do? How were we going to pay our bills? Would my husband be able to get another job considering the economy? All these questions flooded my mind.

I remember grabbing my Bible and going downstairs to spend time talking to Jesus about my concerns. I asked Him to remind me of the truth of who I am in Him and His great love for me. I knew that 1 John 4:18 NKJV says, "Perfect love casts out fear."

As I took my fears to Jesus, He reminded me of the promises I had in Him. I began to say, "Heavenly Father, I don't have to be afraid because I know You love me. You promised to take care of me in difficult times. You said Your plan was to prosper and give me a hope and a future. (Jeremiah 29:11.) I know You love us because You said You'd cause all grace to abound toward us, and we'd have all our needs met in abundance so we can give to every good work."

As I thought about the promises I had in Jesus and remembered that I was abundantly blessed in Him, His perfect love expelled all fear from my heart. The fears subsided, and peace and joy filled my soul. I continued to trust Him and remember the promises He purchased for us. I watched as the Holy Spirit led my husband to start his own business, guided his steps, gave him wisdom, and prospered the work of his hands. In the middle of a bad economy, our income more than doubled, and we had more than enough in the time of famine just like He promised. When you look to Jesus for the grace to trust Him and rest in who you are in Him, you'll experience His plan of abundance for your life.

So the next time you are faced with financial concerns, remember who you are in Jesus. Speak the truth out loud and rest in His unfailing love:

- Jesus loves me. He became poor so that I might be abundantly supplied.
- His grace abounds toward me. I am abundantly blessed because of Jesus.
- I am anointed and empowered to prosper because I am righteous in Jesus.

Prayer

Heavenly Father, I can trust You because You love me. You sent Jesus to take the curse of poverty for me that I might experience Your abundant blessing upon my life. I am blessed when I come in and blessed when I go out. You cause me to have a surplus of prosperity. Your blessing overtakes me. I am anointed and empowered to prosper because You have made me righteous in Christ Jesus.

Day 18

I Am Healed

Surely He has borne our griefs (sicknesses, weaknesses, and distresses) and carried our sorrows and pains [of punishment], yet we [ignorantly] considered Him stricken, smitten, and afflicted by God [as if with leprosy]. But He was wounded for our transgressions, He was bruised for our guilt and iniquities; the chastisement [needful to obtain] peace and well-being for us was upon Him, and with the stripes [that wounded] Him we are healed and made whole.

Isaiah 53:4,5 AMP

Jesus took the punishment of sickness and pain so that you and I could live in divine health. He was bruised for our sins. He obtained peace and wholeness for us. Divine health is part of our inheritance in Christ.

Deuteronomy 28 describes the curse of the law. Under the Old Covenant, curses were the punishment due to the sinner.

> **If you refuse to listen to the LORD your God and do not obey all the commands and decrees I am giving you today, all these curses will come and overwhelm you…. The LORD will afflict you with the boils of Egypt and with tumors, scurvy, and the itch, from which you cannot be cured…. The LORD will afflict you with every sickness and plague there is.**
>
> *Deuteronomy 28:15,27,61 NLT*

Many read this passage of Scripture and come to the conclusion that God makes them sick because of their sin. The devil even uses Scriptures like this to deceive the righteous with these lies: *You deserve to be sick. You're sick because of your sins. God is punishing you.*

But the good news of the Gospel is found in Galatians 3:13,14 NLT:

> **But Christ has rescued us from the curse pronounced by the law. When he was hung**

on the cross, he took upon himself the curse for our wrongdoing. For it is written in the Scriptures, "Cursed is everyone who is hung on a tree." Through Christ Jesus, God has blessed the Gentiles with the same blessing he promised to Abraham, so that we who are believers might receive the promised Holy Spirit through faith.

Jesus redeemed you from every curse of the law by taking the curse for your sins upon Him. He did this so you could live free from the curse of sickness. He has blessed you with the blessing promised to Abraham by making you righteous through your faith in Jesus.

Sickness is a curse upon the sinner, and you're no longer a sinner. You've been made righteous through the blood of Jesus. (Rom. 5:9.) You don't have to accept any sickness in your body.

When I was in my twenties, I had boils, big sores that are very painful and filled with infection, come upon my body. I had to go to the doctor twice to get them lacerated in order to get relief from the pain they caused. Once one would heal, several months later another boil would show up.

I remember one day when I was dealing with another boil and getting very frustrated at why this was happening to me, I asked Jesus to show me the truth that would set me free. I opened my Bible and began to read in Deuteronomy where the curse of the law was listed. When I saw that boils were a curse upon sinners and that Jesus had made me righteous and purchased my freedom from the curse, faith rose up within my heart. I spoke to that boil and commanded it to dry up and never return. I am the righteousness of God in Christ, and I have been redeemed from the curse of the law because Jesus had been cursed for me.

I remember that boil drying up and leaving my body, and I have not had another boil in over ten years. Jesus is our Healer. We are healed in Christ Jesus. We are strong in our spirit, mind, and body because of Him. He paid a great price for us to walk in divine health. All we have to do is believe and agree with who we are in Him. So speak the truth out loud:

- Jesus bore all my sickness and disease; by His stripes I am healed.
- I am redeemed from the curse of the law. Divine health is my inheritance.
- I am righteous in Christ, and I am strong in my spirit, soul, and body.

Prayer

Thank You, Jesus, for redeeming me from the curse of the law by making me righteous in You. You took the punishment for my sins so that I could live free from the curse and enjoy the blessing of God upon my life. I speak to every sickness that would try to come on my body, and I command it to go in Jesus' name. I am the righteousness of God in Christ Jesus, and divine health is my inheritance.

Day 19

I Am Confident

I have told you these things, so that in Me you may have [perfect] peace and confidence. In the world you have tribulation and trials and distress and frustration; but be of good cheer [take courage; be confident, certain, undaunted]! For I have overcome the world.

John 16:33 AMP

Jesus said that He has spoken His words of truth to us so that we can have perfect peace and confidence in this world. On the other hand, the devil speaks his lies to our heart so that we will live in fear. When the trials of life come, He attempts to fill our minds with these fearful thoughts:

Why is this happening to me?
Did I do something wrong?
What if God doesn't come through for me?

Jesus purchased God's promises for us so that we could be confident in every situation. *Confidence* means "freedom from doubt; a feeling of trust (in someone or something); a state of confident hopefulness that events will be favorable."[3] In this world Jesus said that we will have trials and difficult situations to face, but we can have perfect peace in the midst of any storm when we put our confidence in the promise we have in Jesus.

> **So God has given both his promise and his oath. These two things are unchangeable because it is impossible for God to lie. Therefore, we who have fled to him for refuge can have great confidence as we hold to the hope that lies before us. This hope is a strong and trustworthy anchor for our souls.**
>
> *Hebrews 6:18,19 NLT*

Recently I went on cruise with some of my dearest friends. We traveled over a thousand miles together in two vans to get to our port. We were all excited about

---

[3] http://ardictionary.com/Confidence/10173, s.v. "confidence."

spending the week together, and for some it was the first cruise they had ever been on. On our way to the port, we got a call telling us that our departure was going to be delayed due to mechanical problems. This was the first of many delays and unexpected problems that occurred. Our ship ended up being over eight hours late. Many of us were looking forward to vacationing at Cozumel, Mexico, but our destination was changed to someplace much less appealing. There was much distress and frustration all around as things did not turn out as planned.

I remember taking my heart to Jesus and once again asking Him to remind me of who I am in Him and His promise of love for this situation. This verse rose up in my heart:

> **And we know that in all things God works for the good of those who love him, who have been called according to his purpose.**
> *Romans 8:28 NIV*

As I thought about the promise I had in Jesus, perfect peace filled my heart. I had a wonderful vacation because I was confident that God was going to work this all out for our good. His promise was a strong and trustworthy anchor for my soul.

When we returned from our vacation, several weeks later we all received a letter from the company that sponsored the cruise. Due to the inconveniences that we had experienced, we were each offered a free cruise for us and one for our husbands too. I was in awe as I realized that I was able to truly enjoy the first cruise because I placed my confidence in the promise I had in Jesus. Plus, now we would be able to go on another cruise together with our husbands, and it was free! God had truly worked in the situation. Even though there were bumps in the road, He was working behind the scenes to bless us more than we could hope for.

The next time you face a frustrating or difficult situation, remember who you are in Jesus and put your confidence in Him. Speak the truth out loud:

- I am an overcomer in Jesus.
- God is working all things together for my good.
- I am confident in Jesus and the promise I have in Him.

Prayer

Heavenly Father, thank You for showing me that no matter what temptation or trial comes my way, I can be confident in the promise I have in You. You work everything together for my good. You are my refuge and fortress, and I put my confidence in You. I feel secure knowing that nothing can ever separate me from Your love.

Day 20

I Am Changed by God's Grace

But the fruit of the [Holy] Spirit [the work which His presence within accomplishes] is love, joy (gladness), peace, patience…, kindness, goodness…, faithfulness, Gentleness (meekness, humility), self-control.

Galatians 5:22,23 AMP

The Holy Spirit is the Spirit of Grace. In the Amplified Bible, 2 Corinthians 1:12 defines grace as "the unmerited favor and merciful kindness by which God, exerting His holy influence upon souls, turns them to Christ, and keeps, strengthens, and increases them in Christian virtues." You're a righteous, royal child of the King of kings. When you choose to believe the truth of who you are in Jesus, the power of the Spirit of Grace brings out the fruit of godly character in your life. That's why the devil tries so hard to tempt you to believe his lies. He says:

Look at you, you don't look like Jesus.

You don't act like Jesus.

You can't be righteous.

One day while I was watching the movie *The Princess Diaries* with my girls, the Holy Spirit revealed a spiritual truth to me through the movie. The story is about a girl named Mia who was a princess but didn't know it. She felt awkward, ugly, clumsy, and rejected because she had a negative view of herself. Even though Mia was really a princess on the inside, she didn't look like one on the outside because she didn't know who she really was.

One day her grandmother came from a far country to tell Mia that her dad, the king of Genovia, had passed away. That meant that Mia was a princess. She was a member of the royal family. She was an heir to the throne. Everything her daddy had belonged to her.

Mia couldn't believe it. She looked in the mirror and could only see a common girl. She felt like she was not good enough to be a princess. Her grandmother began to teach her how a princess dresses and how a princess acts. Mia tried really hard to do it, but she ended up feeling like a failure. She felt like she'd never measure up to her grandmother's expectations, and she feared that she'd let everyone down. No matter how much her grandmother believed in her, she did not believe the truth about herself. Mia gave up her inheritance because she refused to believe who she really was on the inside.

Then one day she found a letter from her father. He encouraged her to believe the truth about herself. He told her not to let fear hold her back from her destiny. The power to be a princess was within her if she'd only believe.

That day she chose to give up the lies she had believed and instead believe the truth about herself. When she began to see herself as a beautiful, confident, and capable princess, she changed from the inside out. Everyone saw the transformation in her life, and she reigned as the princess of Genovia.

This movie gives a perfect picture of the truth that what you believe about yourself determines the fruit that comes out in your life. I used to believe the lies of the devil. Even though I was a royal princess in the kingdom of God, I had a negative view of myself. Although I had the power of the Spirit of Grace living inside of me, I lived in bondage to fear, insecurity, offence, and condemnation. I didn't experience the fruit of the Spirit because, like many Christians, I didn't really know who I was in Jesus. Just like Mia in *The Princess Diaries*, the fruit of my life didn't reflect who I really was on the inside.

When I began to believe the truth of who I am in Jesus, the Spirit of God began transforming my heart, and I began to see the fruit of the Spirit come out in my life. I became confident and secure in my true identity in Christ.

The same can be true for you. When you choose to believe who you are in Jesus, you'll be changed from the inside out by the Spirit of Grace. You'll reign as a princess in the kingdom of God.

> **You who were once far away from God....**
> **Yet now [God] has reconciled you to**
> **himself through the death of Christ in his**
> **physical body. As a result, he has brought**
> **you into his own presence, and you are**
> **holy and blameless as you stand before**
> **him without a single fault. But you must**
> **continue to believe this truth and stand**
> **firmly in it.**
>
> *Colossians 1:21-23* NLT

So believe who you are in Jesus. Speak the truth out loud:

- I am righteous, valuable, capable, blessed, special, chosen, qualified, favored, approved, adored, and unconditionally loved by the King of kings.

- I am without fault in my Father's eyes because of Jesus.
- I am royalty, and I choose to believe the truth of who I am in Jesus.

Prayer

Heavenly Father, I know You love me because You made me a part of Your royal family. I now understand that it is the Holy Spirit that brings out the fruit in my life when I simply believe who I am in Jesus. Help me to see myself the way You do. I love You, heavenly Father, and I want my life to glorify You.

Day 21

I Am a Minister of Grace

> [It is He] Who has qualified us [making us to be fit and worthy and sufficient] as ministers...of a new covenant [of salvation through Christ], not [ministers] of the letter (of legally written code) but of the Spirit; for the code [of the Law] kills, but the [Holy] Spirit makes alive.
>
> *2 Corinthians 3:6 AMP*

I remember when I felt God calling me to share the good news of the Gospel of Grace with others. The enemy was right there attempting to stop me by speaking his lies to my heart. I remember thinking, *I don't know what to say. I'm not qualified. What if I say something wrong?*

As I talked to Jesus about my fears and concerns, the Holy Spirit reminded me of 2 Corinthians 3:6. Our heavenly Father has qualified us through Jesus. He has equipped us with the wisdom and strength we need to minister His grace to a hurting world.

We're not ministers of the law who tell people what they need to do to be favored and accepted by God. We're ministers of grace who share the good news that through Jesus they are already favored and accepted by Him. We remind believers of who they are in Jesus.

> This means that anyone who belongs to Christ has become a new person. The old life is gone; a new life has begun! And all of this is a gift from God, who brought us back to himself through Christ. And God has given us this task of reconciling people to him. For God was in Christ, reconciling the world to himself, no longer counting people's sins against them. And he gave us this wonderful message of reconciliation. So we are Christ's ambassadors; God is making his appeal through us. We speak for Christ when we plead, "Come back to God!" For God made Christ, who never sinned, to be the offering for our sin, so

that we could be made right with God through Christ.

2 Corinthians 5:17-21 NLT

You've discovered who you are in Jesus. You are royalty, righteous, valuable, and abundantly blessed because of Him. Now God has called you as Christ's ambassador to reconcile others to a personal relationship with Him through Jesus. He has called you to share the good news that Jesus became sin so that others might be made righteous and perfect in God's sight and heirs to all of His promises.

As I have grown in my understanding of who I am in Jesus, God has opened many doors for me to share this good news with others. I've taught ladies' Bible studies in homes and churches. I've written books. I've spoken at ladies' retreats and conferences, and I've been on television sharing the message of grace. In my everyday life I have come across people who are hurting, and the Lord has led me to remind them of who they are in Jesus and the promise they have in Him. There is great satisfaction in being used by God to encourage someone in the Lord. Yet, the enemy of our soul will often speak his lies to our heart to disqualify us or to tempt us to be afraid so that we don't fulfill the call that God has placed on our lives.

In 2007, I received a call from a well-known minister who invited me to come speak at a woman's conference in Russia. I had never been out of the country to minister; I had never spoken through an interpreter; and I had never ministered in front of that many women. I remember being very excited at the honor of being asked to fly across the world as Christ's ambassador to minister the Good News to these precious Russian women. Yet, when I hung up the phone, I remember thinking, *What have I done accepting this invitation? I can't speak through an interpreter. Does she realize how unqualified I am?*

I immediately recognized the feelings of fear that were attacking me and realized that the enemy was aiming his fiery darts at my heart. I turned my thoughts to Jesus and asked Him to help me overcome these negative feelings. He reminded me of who I am in Him. I am anointed and qualified in Jesus to share the Good News with a hurting world. I am capable and sufficient in Jesus. I am Christ's ambassador. As I thought about who I am in Jesus, confidence rose up in my heart.

In March of 2008, I went to Russia, spoke through an interpreter, and shared the good news of the Gospel of Grace with those sweet women. I felt confident that I delivered the message that God had called me to deliver. I witnessed women being set free by the good news of who they are in Jesus and how much He loves them.

You're a minister of God's grace as well. Now that you know who you are in Jesus, you're equipped with everything you need to share the Good News. It may be through writing a book, giving a book away, speaking in front of a group of people, or just sharing the love of Jesus to an individual. You're Christ's ambassador to deliver His message of acceptance and love with others.

When the enemy attempts to stop you by speaking his lies to your heart, remember who you are and agree with the One who loves you. Speak the truth out loud:

- Jesus has anointed and qualified me to minister the good news of the Gospel of Grace.
- I am worthy and sufficient to share His love with others.
- I am Christ's ambassador. I deliver the message of freedom in Jesus to a hurting world.

Prayer

Heavenly Father, thank You for qualifying and equipping me with everything I need to share the Gospel of Grace with others. I am Your ambassador. Use me in my everyday life to tell others of Your love and goodness. I want my life to glorify You.

Prayer of Salvation

God loves you—no matter who you are, no matter what your past. God loves you so much that He gave His one and only begotten Son for you. The Bible tells us "whoever believes in him shall not perish but have eternal life" (John 3:16 NIV). Jesus laid down His life and rose again so that we could spend eternity with Him in heaven and experience His absolute best on earth. If you would like to receive Jesus into your life, say the following prayer out loud and mean it from your heart.

Heavenly Father, I come to You admitting that I am a sinner. Right now, I choose to turn away from sin, and I ask You to cleanse me of all unrighteousness. I believe that Your Son, Jesus, died on the cross to take away my sins. I also believe that He rose again from the dead so that I might be forgiven of my sins and made righteous through faith in Him. I call upon the name of Jesus Christ to be the Savior and Lord of my life. Jesus, I choose to follow You and ask that You fill me with the power of the Holy Spirit. I declare that right now I am a child of God. I am free from sin and full

of the righteousness of God. I am saved in
Jesus' name. Amen.

If you prayed this prayer to receive Jesus Christ as
your Savior for the first time, please contact us on the
web at **www.harrisonhouse.com** to receive a free book.

Or you may write to us at:
Harrison House
P.O. Box 35035
Tulsa, Oklahoma 74153

About the Author

Connie Witter is the founder of Because of Jesus Ministries. She is the author of the Bible study *Because of Jesus* and *P.S. God Loves You.*

Connie has spoken at women's retreats and conferences throughout the U.S. and in Russia. She has been a guest on several Christian television programs and she has her own weekly program, *Because of Jesus,* that airs nationwide to a potential viewing audience of 18 million people. Connie also teaches a weekly ladies' Bible study in her hometown of Broken Arrow, Oklahoma.

The heart of Connie's message is to focus on Jesus and His finished work. Her desire is to empower God's people with the truth of who they are in Jesus. She also encourages them to quit trying to be good enough in their own strength and start resting in the truth that they are already righteous, qualified, favored, dearly loved, and abundantly blessed because of Jesus.

Connie lives in Broken Arrow with her husband of twenty-three years, Tony. God has blessed her with four children, a daughter-in-law, and a granddaughter.

To contact Connie Witter please write to:
Because of Jesus Ministries
P.O. Box 3064
Broken Arrow, OK 74013
Tel: (918) 394-2244
Email: connie@conniewitter.com
Website: www.conniewitter.com

Other Books in the 21 Day Series

21 Days to a Satisfied Life

By Beth Jones

Full of powerful encouragement and amazing ideas for women, this little book will inspire you to find satisfaction in all the right places: A strong relationship with God, a good marriage, godly kids, a place to serve, and purpose for living.

Beth Jones, author of the Getting a Grip on the Basics series, shares with you the secrets to satisfaction from the chic woman of Proverbs 31. In just 21 days you will be encouraged to take steps to lessen stress, make time to know your Father God, and take care of the business of life with planning and patience. Even the craziest days can gain peace and serenity when you live according to God's plan.

978-1-57794-966-4

*Available from bookstores everywhere
or from www.harrisonhouse.com.*

Other Books in the 21 Day Series

21 Days to Your Spiritual Makeover

By Taffi Dollar

With today's busy lifestyles and a world full of distractions, it's easy to lose focus on the One who gave you life to start with. But as you begin to renew your spiritual walk, you will discover the missing peace and joy that brings order to the rest of your day.

Taffi Dollar, popular television co-host, beloved pastor, and esteemed author, helps bring clarity to what is really important in a world of urgent requests. You will see clearly how the beauty of a balanced life brings a calm and joyful attitude to living. Start your spiritual makeover today and begin a beautiful life.

978-1-57794-911-4

*Available from bookstores everywhere
or from www.harrisonhouse.com.*

Fast. Easy.
Convenient.

For the latest Harrison House product infor-
mation and author news, look no further
than your computer. All the details on our
powerful, life-changing products are just a
click away. New releases, E-mail subscriptions,
testimonies, monthly specials—find it all in
one place. Visit harrisonhouse.com today!

harrisonhouse